Born to be Wild
Little Leopards

Ariane Chottin

Words that appear in the glossary are printed in **boldface** type the first time they occur in the text.

An Amazing Acrobat

Even when it is very young, a leopard is a true athlete. Like its mother, a little leopard can leap and perform all kinds of daring **feats**. It knows how to run and climb and has learned how to swim in rivers. Using its claws and strong muscles, it can climb up the surfaces of tall rocks and tree trunks. After climbing to the top of a tree branch, a little leopard can spring like a squirrel from one place to another without missing a single branch.

A mother leopard always keeps an eye on her babies, or cubs. Little leopards are **agile**, courageous, and curious. When a little leopard wanders too far away, its mother gently calls it back to her side.

What do you think?

Why doesn't a mother leopard want her babies to wander off?

a) because they might get lost

b) because she has to protect them from **predators**

c) because she doesn't want them all running off in different directions

A mother leopard doesn't want her babies to wander off because she has to protect them from predators.

A mother leopard has a difficult job protecting her cubs. From the time they are three months old, her cubs follow her everywhere. The cubs learn to hunt by watching and imitating their mother. They also learn to always be aware of danger. Many enemies, especially lions and hyenas, roam the **savanna**. A mother leopard must keep a constant watch, looking for predators and other dangers, to keep her cubs safe.

A little leopard and its brothers and sisters play and fight like kittens. They leap and roll around together, scratch each other with their claws, and gently bite one another on the ears and the tips of their tails.

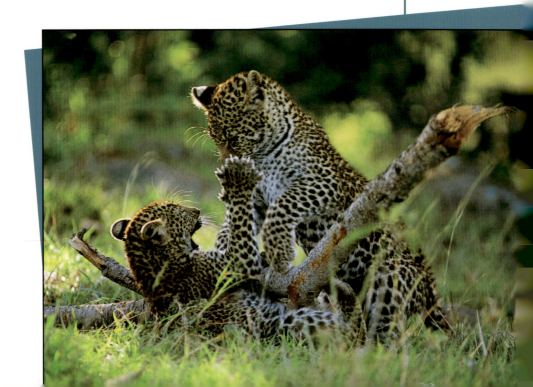

When a mother leopard needs to gather her young, she calls out to them in a fast, high-pitched roar. The cubs answer her with soft mewing sounds.

Young leopards live with their mothers for one and a half to two years. During this time, they learn all the tricks and skills they will need to survive in Africa's savanna. When they are ready, young leopards leave their mothers to begin their own families.

5

Silent Hunters

Little leopards quickly become strong, successful hunters like their mothers. They learn at a young age to walk quietly, putting their paws gently on the ground without making any noise. Young leopards practice catching leaping frogs and other small **prey**, and they are soon able to attack larger animals. The leopards know how to observe, stretching their ears to **detect** the slightest noises, the weakest cracklings, and the sounds of the smallest movements in the grass.

What do you think?

How does a leopard attack its prey?

a) It frightens the prey.

b) It chases the prey.

c) It approaches the prey as closely and quietly as possible without being detected.

Leopards usually hunt alone, but they sometimes gather together to hunt. One of them, for example, will climb a tree to scare monkeys perched on its branches, while the rest of the leopards wait at the base of the tree to capture the monkeys as they try to escape.

A leopard attacks its prey by approaching it as closely and quietly as possible without being detected.

When it is time to hunt, a leopard waits patiently, staying as still as a statue. Then it moves very slowly, creeping soundlessly on its padded paws through the tall grasses. When it is very close to its prey, the leopard stops and waits for the right moment to strike. It is so close that it can reach its victim in a single leap.

A leopard hunts only for food. When it captures a large animal, it hauls the carcass to a place as high off the ground as possible, usually onto a strong tree branch. The branch is a kind of "safe" that is very difficult for most other animals to reach.

When a young leopard becomes an adult, it will eat all kinds of prey. Like its parents, it will eat gazelles, monkeys, and squirrels, plus eggs, fruits, and, sometimes, even a fish that it has caught by itself.

During the dry season, water is scarce, and a leopard must sometimes go for weeks without drinking. When it finally discovers a small pond, the leopard takes all the time it needs to satisfy its thirst.

A Royal Robe

At birth, a little leopard is covered with brown fur that is as smooth and velvety as a child's soft toy animal. Some weeks later, spots appear on the little leopard's coat, turning it into a robe fit for royalty. The spots are called rosettes. Each rosette is made up of two to four dark points surrounding a patch of fur that is darker than the rest of the coat.

The base color of a leopard's fur varies according to the region in which the leopard lives. Sometimes, the fur is a reddish color, and sometimes, it is gray or yellow, but the color on a leopard's belly and the underside of its paws is always white or light yellow.

What do you think?

Why is a leopard's coat spotted?

a) because a spotted coat provides **camouflage**

b) because its parents were a black leopard and a light-colored leopard

c) because leopards want to be the most beautiful big cats

11

A leopard's coat is spotted to provide camouflage in the wild.

With its spotted coat, a leopard is able to blend into the light-colored grasses of the African savanna and move around **virtually** unnoticed. Its coat is a perfect camouflage! Other big cats, such as jaguars and cheetahs, also have fur coats that are sprinkled with small, dark spots. Unlike a leopard's spots, however, a cheetah's spots are small, round, and solid black, and a jaguar's spots are large rosettes with a brown center.

The famous and beautiful black leopards live in Asia. They have spots on their dark coats, but the spots are nearly invisible. A black leopard's spots can be seen only close-up.

Snow leopards, which live in the mountains of central Asia, have thick white and gray fur with dark spots. They also have long, tufted tails that they coil around themselves like warm scarves when they sleep.

Clouded leopards are related to African leopards. These cats are also called long-banded leopards because of the six dark bands of color on their fur. Their coats help clouded leopards blend into the forests of Indonesia and India, which is where they live.

Velvet Paws

A little leopard can move without making a sound because the bottoms of its paws have flexible cushions. Between the cushions, and between the leopard's toes, are soft, fine hairs that absorb or smother the sounds of the animal's movements. A leopard also has large, scary claws that are as sharp as a knife's edge. Its sharp claws spring from a little leopard's velvet paws when it is climbing or attacking prey.

What do you think?

How many teeth does a leopard have?

a) twenty long teeth

b) thirty well-sharpened teeth

c) forty-five pointed teeth

A leopard's head has short, stiff hair and long, **quivering** whiskers. Its sensitive whiskers allow a leopard to feel or detect the objects around it, which helps the animal move quickly on even the darkest nights.

A leopard has thirty well-sharpened teeth. At the age of five months, a little leopard's baby teeth fall out and its adult teeth grow in. The cub's days of eating meat **regurgitated** by its mother are over! Thanks to its new, sharp teeth, the little leopard can begin to devour prey on its own. A leopard has thirty teeth. With sharp canines for holding prey, incisors for biting, and premolars and molars for sawing, it has the perfect set of teeth for eating raw meat.

Leopards have the largest eyes of any carnivore. Their round pupils can widen quickly, allowing the animals to see very well in the dark. Leopards can see about seven times better than humans.

A leopard has good ears and can hear two or three times better than a human.

A little leopard's tongue is covered with small, hornlike bumps. Its raspy tongue is the perfect tool for licking bones clean at the end of a meal. A bumpy tongue also comes in handy for grooming.

All Grown Up

When they reach adulthood, leopards leave their mothers and other family members to live alone. The young adults must travel long distances to find territories of their own. Every day, each leopard roams in large circles, exploring its new home, establishing boundaries, and hunting prey. When mating season arrives, males and females meet and choose mates to begin their own families. Each pair of leopards then roams its territory together.

When a leopard meets its mate, the two stay together. They sleep together and take turns grooming each other. They also hunt together and share the captured prey.

What do you think?

What type of shelter does a leopard choose for its babies?

a) a quiet corner in the grasses of the savanna

b) a den dug into the earth

c) a hole in a tree or rock

A leopard uses a hole in a tree or rock as a shelter for its babies.

Three months after mating, the female leopard searches for a place that will be a safe home for her young. Soon after, she gives birth to a litter of two, three, or four cubs. The little leopards are as small as kittens and covered with dark fur. Their eyes remain closed for ten days. Right away, however, the hungry babies begin to drink their mother's milk, purring contentedly.

A mother leopard spends lots of time grooming her cubs. She takes great care with their coats, licking the cubs over and over, from the points of their small ears to the tips of their tails.

A mother leopard feeds her cubs milk for two or three months. The cubs' father brings her food during this time — fresh prey that he has caught.

As soon as little leopards are **weaned**, the mother and father separate. The female continues to raise her young alone, feeding them regurgitated meat, at first, and later, bringing them small, live prey. The male leopard returns to his own territory and lives alone until the next mating season.

Leopards are **mammals** that, in the wild, live in the savannas of Africa as well as in the mountains, deserts, and rain forests of Africa, southwestern Asia, and China. Adult leopards can weigh up to 140 pounds (65 kilograms) and live about twenty years, in the wild.

There are twenty-four kinds of leopards. They are members of the same family as lions, tigers, and jaguars and are related to all cats — even house cats.

A leopard has excellent hearing and can detect sounds humans cannot hear.

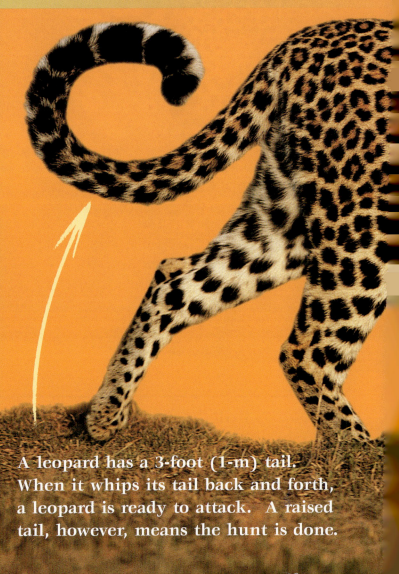

A leopard has a 3-foot (1-m) tail. When it whips its tail back and forth, a leopard is ready to attack. A raised tail, however, means the hunt is done.

A leopard measures 6 to 9 feet (2 to 3 meters) from its head to the tip of its tail.

A leopard's eyes are very large and set close together. The pupils can get larger or smaller very quickly, allowing the animal to see well in the dark.

The round ears of a leopard, like the ears of a small house cat, move toward the sounds it hears.

A leopard's whiskers are long, stiff, and very sensitive. They help the animal sense or feel obstacles in its path, even in the dark.

A leopard's muscular paws are like strong springs. The length of the animal's stride is about 13 to 20 feet (4 to 6 m).

GLOSSARY

agile — able to move quickly, lightly, and easily

camouflage — a pattern or color that helps something blend in with its surroundings

carcass — an animal's dead body

carnivore — an animal that eats the flesh of other animals; a meat eater

detect — discover or notice

feats — acts that show skill, strength, or bravery

mammals — warm-blooded animals that have backbones, give birth to live babies, feed their young with milk from the mother's body, and have skin that is usually covered with hair or fur

predators — animals that hunt and kill other animals for food

prey — animals that are hunted and killed by a predator

quivering — shaking with a slight vibrating motion

regurgitated — brought back up into the mouth after being chewed and swallowed

savanna — a large, flat area of grassland with scattered trees, found in warm parts of the world

virtually — almost entirely

weaned — able to eat other foods besides milk

Please visit our web site at: www.garethstevens.com
For a free color catalog describing Gareth Stevens Publishing's list of high-quality books and multimedia programs, call 1-800-542-2595 (USA) or 1-800-387-3178 (Canada). Gareth Stevens Publishing's fax: (414) 332-3567.

Library of Congress Cataloging-in-Publication Data

Chottin, Ariane.
  [Petite panthère. English]
  Little leopards / Ariane Chottin. — North American ed.
     p. cm. — (Born to be wild)
  ISBN 0-8368-4438-6 (lib. bdg.)
  1. Leopard—Infancy—Juvenile literature. I. Title. II. Series.
  QL737.C23C4813   2005
  599.75'54139—dc22   2004059726

This North American edition first published in 2005 by
Gareth Stevens Publishing
A WRC Media Company
330 West Olive Street, Suite 100
Milwaukee, Wisconsin 53212 USA

This U.S. edition copyright © 2005 by Gareth Stevens, Inc.
Original edition copyright © 2001 by Mango Jeunesse.

First published in 2001 as *La petite panthère* by Mango Jeunesse, an imprint of Editions Mango, Paris, France.
Picture Credits (t=top, b=bottom, l=left, r=right)
Bios: H. Van den Berg title page, 5(t); N. Granier 9(b), 17(b); M. and C. Denis-Huot 10, back cover; CI. Thouvenin 14; A. Pons 18. Colibri: A. M. Loubsens 17(t), 22-23. Jacana: A. Shap 2, 3, 4, 5(b), 6, 7, 8, 9(t), 11, 15, 16, 19, 20(both), 21, 22(l); M.C. Hugh 13(b); Sylvain Cordier 12. Phone: J. P. Ferrero cover. Sunset: G. Lacz 13(t).

English translation: Pat Lantier
Gareth Stevens editor: Barbara Kiely Miller
Gareth Stevens art direction: Tammy West

All rights reserved. No part of this book may be reproduced, stored in a retrieval system, or transmitted in any form or by any means, electronic, mechanical, photocopying, recording, or otherwise, without the prior written permission of the copyright holder.

Printed in the United States of America

1 2 3 4 5 6 7 8 9 09 08 07 06 05